Sinatra

Sinatra

Tim Frew

press
élan

First Published in Canada in 1998 by
élan press, an imprint of General Publishing Co. Limited
30 Lesmill Road
Toronto, Canada
M3B 2T6
(416) 445-3333

Canadian Cataloguing in Publication Data
available from the National Library of Canada

ISBN 1-55144-198-5

Sinatra
was prepared and produced by
Michael Friedman Publishing Group, Inc.
15 West 26th Street
New York, New York 10010
USA

Editor: Francine Hornberger
Art Director: Kevin Ullrich
Designers: Robert Brook Allen and Millie Sensat
Photography Editor: Deidra Gorgos
Production Manager: Ingrid Neimanis-McNamara

Printed in the United States

Dedication

For my mother, who helped instill in me my love for music.

Acknowledgments

I would like to thank my editor Francine Hornberger for her patience and guidance, Deidra Gorgos for unearthing these great photos of Frank, and designer Robert Brook Allen for turning the words and pictures into a book. I would also like to thank my wife, Susanne Frank, for being there when I needed her.

CONTENTS

Introduction

Above: Hollywood was quick to tap into the "Frankie" phenomenon. Sinatra became a popular movie star in the 1940s, appearing in thirteen films. Here, Frank reviews a script.

Opposite: In his early career, Sinatra appealed to young audiences with his casual style and his signature bow-ties. "I wear bow-ties, sports jackets and sweaters, and kids like 'em," explained Sinatra in a 1943 *Life* magazine article. "I'm their type."

On December 30, 1942, a gangly, big-eared, twenty-seven-year-old singer with a curl of dark hair straggling across his forehead stood in the wings of the Paramount in New York City, fiddling with his bow-tie as he waited to be introduced. Frank Sinatra was billed as an "Added Extra Attraction" in a New Year's engagement headlined by The King of Swing, Benny Goodman. It was the most important engagement of Sinatra's fledgling solo career.

But Sinatra was not a complete unknown back then. He had spent nearly three years as the featured vocalist for the Tommy Dorsey band, with whom he recorded such hits as "I'll Never Smile Again" (1940), "Delores" (1941), and "There Are Such Things" (1942). In 1941, he was voted outstanding male vocalist in both *Billboard* and *Downbeat* polls. In Benny Goodman's eyes, however, Sinatra was just one of countless singers trying to make a name for himself. So when the time came for the "skinny kid from Hoboken" to grace the stage, an unimpressed Goodman introduced him with a curt, "And now, Frank Sinatra." With that, the largely bobbysoxer audience exploded in hysteria. "The sound that greeted me was absolutely deafening," Sinatra later recalled. "It was a tremendous roar....I couldn't move a muscle. Benny froze too....He turned around, looked at the audience and asked, 'What the hell is that?' I burst out laughing and gave out with 'For Me and My Gal.'"

Sinatra's initial four-week engagement was extended to ten weeks. Long after Benny Goodman and his band left the bill, Sinatra continued to pack the house with enthusiastic audiences, mostly comprised of young girls who screamed and swooned at his every inflection. Never before had a singer elicited such excitement and pandemonium from an audience. Just a few years before, Sinatra had been singing and waiting tables at the Rustic Cabin in Englewood, New Jersey, for fifteen dollars a week. By the end of his stint at the Paramount, he was earning $1,250 a week, and his career was rolling along better than anyone could have imagined. After the Paramount, Frank signed deals with the *Your Hit Parade* radio show, RKO Pictures, and Columbia Records. Sinatra became known alternately as "The Voice that Thrilled Millions," "The Sultan of Swoon," "Frankie," or, most commonly, "The Voice." Later nicknames included "The Chairman of the Board" and "Ol' Blue Eyes."

Not even World War II could get in his way. Sinatra was not drafted, declared 4-F because of a punctured eardrum he suffered at birth. (The doctor delivered him using forceps, which also caused scarring around Frank's face and neck). Many people attributed Sinatra's huge popularity with female fans to a "mass hysteria" caused by a lack of young men at home. Sinatra later admitted, "It was the war years, and there was a great loneliness. And I was the boy in every corner drug store...who'd gone off, drafted to the war. That's all." Sinatra's 1940 recording of "I'll Be Seeing You" with Tommy Dorsey became a major hit after Pearl Harbor, when its lyric took on special significance for soldiers going off to war.

Left: With the "bobby-soxer" 1940s behind him and his career in a shambles, Frank Sinatra made one of the greatest comebacks in pop music history in the 1950s. With sophisticated arrangements and jazz-influenced vocal phrasing, Frank appealed to a more adult audience with a series of albums that became known as "the fabulous sixteen."

Many resented Sinatra's rising fame, while American soldiers were laying down their lives overseas. In an effort to diffuse the negative publicity, Frank's press agent, George Evans, booked the singer for as many war bond rallies as possible. Publicly, Frank expressed disappointment that he was ineligible for military service. Privately, he was happy that he didn't have to put his career on hold—and lose out on nearly a half a million dollars in contracts. "From the first minute I walked on a stage," Sinatra told a reporter, "I [was] determined to get exactly where I am; like a guy who starts out being an office boy but has a vision of occupying the president's office...."

Francis Albert Sinatra was born on December 12, 1915, in Hoboken, New Jersey. His mother, Dolly, was a Democratic ward leader who wielded substantial power in Hoboken political circles, and his father, Marty, was a former professional boxer (who fought under the name "Marty O'Brien") who became a tavern owner and firefighter. "In my particular neighborhood of New Jersey," Sinatra once said, "boys became boxers or they worked in factories, and then the remaining group that I went around with were smitten by singing. I mean, we had a ukulele player, and we'd stand on the corner and sing songs."

Singers were always Frank's biggest idols; his childhood room was papered with photographs of Al Jolson, Rudy Vallee, and Bing Crosby. Sinatra sang in the Demarest High School glee club and played in the band, but he dropped out of high school at the age of

sixteen. At eighteen he took his girlfriend—and future wife—Nancy Barbato to see Bing Crosby perform at a local vaudeville theater. "I never saw anyone sit so still as Frank did that evening," recalled Nancy. "When we came out of the theater, he said, 'That is what I want to do.'"

In 1934, Sinatra auditioned for the *Major Bowes Original Amateur Hour,* a national radio talent contest, which was the most popular radio show in the United States at the time. Here, he met up with the other members of what would become "The Hoboken Four." Sinatra and the band were enthusiastically received by the studio audience and won first prize for their performance. After the performance, Sinatra uttered his first words on live radio: "I'm Frank, Major. We're looking for jobs. How about it? Everybody that's ever heard us likes us. We think we're pretty good."

Bowes did give them work, first a one-week engagement at the Roxy and then three months on the road with the *Amateur Hour* touring company. After the tour, Frank left the group and began singing solo at taverns, weddings, social clubs, virtually any place that would have him. In 1937, his mother got him his job at the Rustic Cabin. The shows were broadcast on the radio live every night on WNEW New York. "We used to be on the air on [a] thing called 'The WNEW Dance Parade' in New York," recalled Sinatra. "They'd pick up little roadhouses and nightclubs, and we had fifteen minutes on the air...five nights a week. And that, of course, was very important to me, because people were beginning to hear me."

One person who heard Sinatra sing was bandleader Harry James. Just four months earlier James had left Benny Goodman—where he was the star trumpet player—to form his own band, and he was looking for a lead singer. After hearing Sinatra on the radio, James went to see him firsthand. "This very thin guy with swept-back greasy hair had been waiting tables," recalled James. "Suddenly he took off his apron and climbed onto the stage. He'd sung only eight bars when I felt the hairs on the back of my neck rising. I knew he was destined to be a great vocalist."

James signed Sinatra to a two-year contract in 1939. Frank sang in his first concert with James at the Hippodrome in Baltimore and made his first recording, "From the Bottom of My Heart," on July 13 that same year. Sinatra honored only six months of his two-year commitment before signing on with Tommy Dorsey. The notoriously good-hearted James let Frank out of his contract without any hassles. Dorsey was not so understanding a few years later, however, when Frank wanted to leave *his* band and go solo. After tense negotiations and a considerable amount of money paid to Dorsey, Sinatra was released from the contract—the split forever ending their friendship.

No one could have predicted just how much of an impact the singer would have on the world of popular music, and on American popular culture as a whole. Many music critics in the 1940s were convinced that the "Frankie" phenomenon was just a fad and that Sinatra would be finished as soon as the war was over and the GIs came home. They were almost correct. Sinatra's star had fallen by the early 1950s. His career finally started looking up again, when he won an Oscar for his performance as Maggio in *From Here to Eternity* (1953)—a role for which he had to lobby hard just to get an audition.

With his career now showing new signs of life, Sinatra signed with Capitol Records and teamed up with a young arranger named Nelson Riddle. Riddle played trombone for Tommy Dorsey and arranged songs for Nat King Cole ("Mona Lisa" [1950], "Too Young" [1951]). His tight swinging arrangements fit perfectly with Sinatra's style of song interpretation. The young innovative arranger knew that a Sinatra song must tell a story and that the arrangements must serve to push that story along. He also brought elements of jazz into Sinatra's singing. And Sinatra's perfectionism, in turn, rubbed off on Riddle.

"Working with Frank was always a challenge," said Riddle. "Never a relaxed man, as Nat Cole was, for example, he was a perfectionist who drove himself and everybody around him relentlessly....He showed me how to insist on certain things from an orchestra, so I guess you could say I learned from Frank like he learned from me." Their first recording together was "I've Got the World on a String," an ironic choice, considering Frank's

Opposite: Throughout his career, Sinatra tended to surrounded himself with an entourage of friends, associates, starlets, models, mobsters, bodyguards, handlers, and various hangers-on, yet he remained an intensely private person who would often seem terribly lonely even in the liveliest crowd. "Being an eighteen-karat manic depressive," Sinatra once said, "I have an over-acute capacity for sadness as well as elation."

career was at an all-time low. Yet, it helped usher in a new era in Sinatra's career, and in popular music in general. Unlike in the forties, Frank was now making music for adults. The Sinatra/Riddle team was geared toward album-length projects; *In the Wee Small Hours* (1955) was one of the first concept albums ever recorded.

Sinatra made more than 600 recordings with Capitol from 1954 to 1962 before starting his own label, Reprise. While he charted few top singles ("Young at Heart" [1954]; "Learnin' the Blues" [1955]; "Hey Jealous Lover," [1956]; "All the Way" [1957]; and "Witchcraft" [1958]), nearly all of his fourteen albums during that time reached the top five on the *Billboard* album chart. On such albums as *In the Wee Small Hours*, *Songs for Swingin' Lovers* (1956), *A Swingin' Affair* (1957), and *Come Fly with Me* (1958), Sinatra's voice is at its best: warm and woody with easy, conversational phrasing. In *Sinatra, An American Classic* (Random House, 1984), author John Rockwell writes: "Sinatra's singing...has a verve and conviction that make his records from the forties sound bland. He has learned to tease and twist a vocal line without violating its integrity."

In the late 1950s, Sinatra put Las Vegas on the map as an entertainment Mecca. In his notorious performances at the Sands with the "Rat Pack"—Dean Martin, Sammy Davis, Jr., Peter Lawford, and Joey Bishop—he defined the image of the hard-drinking, swinging, cool, Vegas jokester. The Rat Pack, which Sinatra preferred to refer to as "The Summit," had its own club house (the steam room at the Sands); its own language ("bird" for penis, "Charlies" for breasts, "gas" for fun, "in the big Casino" for death, "The big G" for God, and "Dullsville, Ohio" for anyplace but Las Vegas); and an undisputed, omnipotent leader, Frank Sinatra. If Sinatra was bored with a particular night club, he would simply say, "I think it's going to rain," and that was the cue for the group to leave. And no one in the Rat Pack

was allowed to go to bed before Sinatra, which usually meant well past dawn. Frank's favorite color was "Five O'Clock Vegas Blue," the color of the Vegas sky just before sunrise.

Sinatra was forever making comebacks. His love life, alleged Mob connections, and angry public outbursts fed a press corps constantly hungry for scandal. His public battles—especially with the press—were the stuff of legend. Sinatra regularly sent threatening telegrams to gossip columnists who wrote negative things about him. And his notorious drinking and womanizing made him a frequent victim of particularly nasty notices in the tabloids.

Yet for all of his arrogance, Sinatra could also be an extremely kind and generous man. He dedicated his time to countless causes—fighting especially hard against racial intolerance. Noël Coward wrote that Sinatra was a "remarkable personality—tough, vulnerable, and somehow touching. He is also immeasurably kind." Sammy Davis, Jr., who lost his eye in an auto accident, credited Sinatra for pulling him out of his depression.

In a career that touched seven decades, Frank Sinatra proved himself to be the greatest pop singer of all time. At his best, he sang with an emotion so strong that it seemed as if each song was a personal statement made directly to the listener. He was the prototypical pop singer, yet he phrased his songs like a jazz improviser. Jazz legend Miles Davis stated that many of his solos were played the way he would have imagined Frank Sinatra singing them. Once Frank sang a song, it became his and his alone—no matter how many other artists put their versions to tape. "They Can't Take that Away from Me," "I Get a Kick Out of You," "Fly Me to the Moon," "Night and Day," "My Funny Valentine," these are all standards of American popular music, recorded countless numbers of times, yet they are all inextricably linked with the legend of Frank Sinatra.

Chapter One

The Early Years

Above: Francis Albert Sinatra, age three. Sinatra was born in his parents' Hoboken apartment. The difficult birth nearly resulted in the death of both mother and son. In fact, Frank was at first thought stillborn and only burst to life after his grandmother held him under cold running water. Dolly, who was twenty years old, survived, but could have no more children.

Opposite: Frank Sinatra's parents, Anthony Martin and Natalie "Dolly" Sinatra on their wedding day, February 14, 1914. Dolly's parents didn't approve of the union between their daughter and the young boxer and refused to throw them a wedding, so the two went to City Hall in Jersey City and got married on their own.

Above: A young Frank Sinatra (front row, far right) during a family vacation at Echo Farm in the Catskill Mountains, upstate New York, 1923.

Above: Dolly Sinatra and a thirteen-year-old Frank. A very determined woman, Dolly was often out of the house working at her husband's saloon, at a chocolate factory, or making her rounds as a Democratic ward leader. "I wanted a girl and bought a lot of pink clothes," she once said. "When Frank was born, I didn't care. I dressed him in pink anyway." As a young boy Frank had such an extensive wardrobe that his friends called him "Slacksey O'Brien."

Right: Sinatra, far right, with his first professional singing group, The Hoboken Four, after appearing on the *Major Bowes Amateur Hour* radio show in 1935. The quartet sang the Mills Brothers' arrangement of "Shine" (a recording of which still exists). Response to the group was so enthusiastic that the Major signed them up to become part of his touring company.

ight: While touring as the main singer for Harry James and His Music Makers, Frank heard that Tommy Dorsey was looking for a young male singer to replace Jack Leonard, one of the most popular band singers of the era who was looking to turn to a solo career. "I wanted to sing with Dorsey more than anything else," Sinatra later admitted. Frank slipped Dorsey a note and set up an audition. He sang "Marie," a Jack Leonard signature song and one of Dorsey's biggest hits, and was hired for $125 per week. Here, Sinatra, back row far right, poses with Tommy Dorsey, front row far right, on the set of the movie *Las Vegas Nights*, 1941.

Opposite: Frank and Tommy Dorsey record a song at the RCA Victor Studios in New York City, 1941. "I learned about dynamics and phrasing and style from the way he played his horn," Sinatra said of Tommy Dorsey. "[He] was a real education to me...in music, in business, in every possible way."

Above: Frank Sinatra made a modest movie debut in 1941, when he appeared with Dorsey and his orchestra in *Las Vegas Nights.* He didn't have a speaking part, but sang "I'll Never Smile Again," his first big hit with Dorsey. That same year Sinatra was named the outstanding male band vocalist in both *Billboard* and *Downbeat* magazines, replacing Bing Crosby in the number-one slot.

Chapter Two

The Sultan of Swoon

Opposite: Sinatra got his first big break when he played a New Year's show with Benny Goodman. When Frank walked out onto the stage, he was greated by a cacophony of screams from the bobbysoxer audience. "The sound that greeted me was absolutely deafening," recalled Sinatra. "It was a tremendous roar...I was scared stiff...." Here, Goodman, left, and Sinatra play the "switcheroo" with a bespectacled Frank on clarinet and Benny behind the mike.

Above: Following his success at the Paramount, Frank signed deals with Columbia Records, RKO, and *Your Hit Parade.* Suddenly the gawky kid from Hoboken was one of the most famous—and well paid—performers in America. "I'm in the $100,000 class now," he told the New York *Daily News.* Always a keen self-promoter, here Frank autographs records for Columbia.

Above: After two and a half years, two movies, thirty-six recording sessions, countless tour dates, and six number-one hits with Tommy Dorsey, Frank Sinatra decided he wanted to make it on his own. He headed to California to conquer the West Coast. Here, Frank is greeted by throngs of screaming fans at the Pasadena train station on August 11, 1943, before his sold-out show at the Hollywood Bowl.

Above: Five thousand fans met Sinatra at the Pasadena train station. RKO had arranged for him to disembark there instead of in Los Angeles to avoid a possible riot, but began to worry that no fans would greet Frank, so it leaked the time and location of his arrival to local radio stations.

Left: Sinatra belts out a song in *Higher and Higher* (1943), which provided his first starring role. He played a "boy next door" character. "I Couldn't Sleep A Wink Last Night" was one of the hit songs to come out of the film.

Right: Frank Sinatra listens to a playback of a scene from *Higher and Higher* (1943). While the film was a box-office smash, critics had mixed reactions to Frank's first attempts at a lead role. *The New York Times* dubbed the film "Lower and Lower" and declared that "Frankie is no Gable or Barrymore." *The New York Herald-Tribune* reported that Frank "does his stint remarkably well for a comparative novice. His ugly, bony face photographs well; his voice registers agreeably enough on microphone, and he handles himself easily..."

Left: Frank is welcomed back to New York by his wife, Nancy, and three-year-old daughter, Nancy Sandra, after completing the filming of *Higher and Higher,* September 23, 1943. By this time, Frank's relentless schedule and his womanizing had already put a severe strain on his marriage of four years.

Opposite: Frank shows he's light on his feet during a rehearsal for the *Your Hit Parade* radio show, 1943. Sinatra succeeded Barry Wood as the featured vocalist on this influential national radio show, which counted down the top hits of the day. His first broadcast was on February 6, 1943.

Above: Sinatra in a scene from *Step Lively,* a 1944 musical version of the Marx Brother's 1938 hit, *Room Service*. In this movie, Frank received his first film kisses, from Gloria DeHaven and Anne Jeffreys. During the filming, Nancy gave birth to the couple's second child, Frank, Jr., on January 10, 1944. Frank was not present for the birth, just as he had not been present for the birth of Nancy Sandra four years earlier.

Left: Sinatra reviews the music before a CBS radio broadcast in 1944. That same year Sinatra signed a five-year, $1.5 million contract with MGM, making him one of the highest-paid entertainers in the world at the time.

Right: Frank clowns around, pretending to be a conductor during a recording session at a CBS studio, 1944. Despite appearances in this photo, Sinatra was extremely serious, and sometimes tyrannical, during his recording sessions. "Once you're on that record singing," he explained, "it's you and you alone. If it's bad and gets you criticized, it's you who's to blame—no one else. If it's good, it's also you."

Right: Frank and Nancy during a night out at the Trocadero in Hollywood, February 2, 1945. Frank decided that he loved California and didn't want to return to Hoboken, so he bought Mary Astor's estate in Toluca Lake and moved Nancy and their two children out to the West Coast. Nancy was still incredulous about her husband's success: "All I could think of was the time six years ago when I had spaghetti without meat sauce because meat sauce was more expensive. And now Frank has made a million in a year!"

Opposite: Frank rehearsed for eight weeks with Gene Kelly to learn the dance steps for *Anchors Aweigh* (1945). Frank credited Kelly for teaching him how to act, how to dance, and how to use his entire body while performing.

Above: Sinatra using his charm in *Anchors Aweigh* (1945). Sinatra had one of his notorious blowups on the set, declaring, "Pictures stink and most of the people in them do too. Hollywood won't believe I'm through, but they'll find out I mean it...." The next day he issued an apology: "It's easy for a guy to get hot under the collar, literally and figuratively, when he's dressed in a hot suit of Navy blues and the temperature is a hundred and four degrees....I think I might have spoken too broadly about quitting pictures and about my feelings toward Hollywood."

Frank was always quick to speak out in favor of liberal social causes, campaigning especially hard for racial tolerance. In 1945, he made a short subject film devoted to the theme of tolerance called *The House I Live In*, for which he received a special Oscar. In these two photographs, Frank speaks to groups of high school students, warning them of the dangers of hurling racial epithets. The singer said, "If you have to call someone a name, don't put a racial prefix in front of it."

Above: Frank, mugging in the background, with, from left to right, Bette Davis, Jose Iturbi, Jimmy Durante, and Bing Crosby (Frank's boyhood signing idol) during a rehearsal for "Command Performance," the Armed Forces Radio Service V-J Day Show in August 1945.

Left: In 1946, Frank left his wife Nancy and temporarily moved out of their Toluca Lake home. A few days later, Frank was seen dancing with Ava Gardner and dining with Lana Turner in Palm Springs. Then, just a few weeks after the separation, Frank joined Phil Silvers on stage at a Hollywood club. During a rendition of "Going Home," Frank looked up and saw a tearful Nancy in the audience. Here, the happily reconciled couple are shown leaving the club.

A bove: Frank seated with Eleanor Roosevelt at a Girls Town benefit at the Fountainbleu in Miami Beach, Florida. Sinatra was an ardent admirer of the liberal former first lady.

R ight: Sinatra waits for his cue to start his song, "Ol' Man River," during the filming of 'Till the Clouds Roll By (1946). Frank made a special guest appearance in this biopic about composer Jerome Kern. The film also featured the talents of Judy Garland, Angela Lansbury, Lena Horne, Dinah Shore, and Tony Martin.

Opposite: By the end of the 1940s, Sinatra's career was on the sharp decline. His womanizing and regular public outbursts made him an easy and frequent target of the Hollywood gossip press. On April 8, 1947, Sinatra—angered by Lee Mortimer's negative review of *It Happened in Brooklyn,* and by the reporter's public allegations of Mob connections—beat up the diminutive columnist (shown in the background) outside Ciro's, a Hollywood nightclub.

Above: *The Kissing Bandit* (1948) was another Sinatra bomb. *The New York Times* wrote, "Except for appearing gawky, which seems not very hard for him to do, and singing the Nacio Herb Brown songs rather nicely, he contributes little."

Left: In a role that sharply contrasted with his off-screen reputation, Sinatra played a priest opposite Fred MacMurray in the 1948 film *The Miracle of the Bells*. The movie was a critical and commercial flop, causing RKO and MGM to question the future of Sinatra's movie career.

Opposite and Above: In 1949, MGM attempted to rescue Sinatra's faltering movie career by teaming him up with Gene Kelly for *Take Me Out to the Ball Game* and *On the Town*, in the hopes that the two could repeat their success in 1945's *Anchors Aweigh*. Both films were well received by critics and audiences alike.

Right: A happy Frank poses with his first daughter, Nancy, to Frank's left, his wife Nancy, daughter Tina, and Frank, Jr. Despite efforts by Nancy to save her marriage, Frank continued his infidelity, in 1949 with Lana Turner and with rising screen actress Ava Gardner in 1950. His relationship with Ava would cause the Sinatras to divorce.

Above: Sinatra and Gardner at the opening of a two-week singing engagement in Las Vegas, Nevada, in 1951. Both Frank and Ava were still married at the time, Ava to bandleader Artie Shaw. Frank was in Nevada to complete a two-week residency requirement in order to obtain a divorce from Nancy.

Left: Six days after his divorce from Nancy became official, Frank married Ava in Germantown, Pennsylvania, on November 7, 1951. The two had a very passionate yet tumultuous relationship that ended in divorce just six years later. Frank always maintained that Ava was the true love of his life.

Right: By 1952, Frank Sinatra's life and career were in turmoil. He had been dropped by MGM; his longtime press agent George Evans had died unexpectedly at the age of forty-eight; his latest movie, *Meet Danny Wilson* (1952, shown at right), had been a commercial flop, leading Universal to cancel the second picture of a two-picture deal; he had been dropped by Columbia Records; CBS television canceled *The Frank Sinatra Show* (which ran from October 1950 to April 1952); and he had been dropped by his theatrical agency. It seemed as if Sinatra's career had finally hit the skids.

Chapter Three

From Here to Eternity

Opposite: Frank and Ava rally in support of Adlai Stevenson at the Palladium Ballroom in Hollywood, October 27, 1952. More then four thousand people attended the event as Ava introduced her husband before he sang "The Birth of the Blues" and "The House I Live In." Less than two weeks earlier, the couple had separated after a particularly violent row at their Palm Springs home involving Ava, Frank, and Lana Turner.

Above: Sinatra won the Best Supporting Actor Oscar for his role as Maggio in *From Here to Eternity* (1953). Here, he kisses his costar and the Best Supporting Actress award winner Donna Reed. Sinatra later ducked out of a post-Oscar party to take a walk and reflect on his remarkable comeback. "Just me and Oscar! I think I relived my entire lifetime that night as I walked up and down the streets of Beverly Hills."

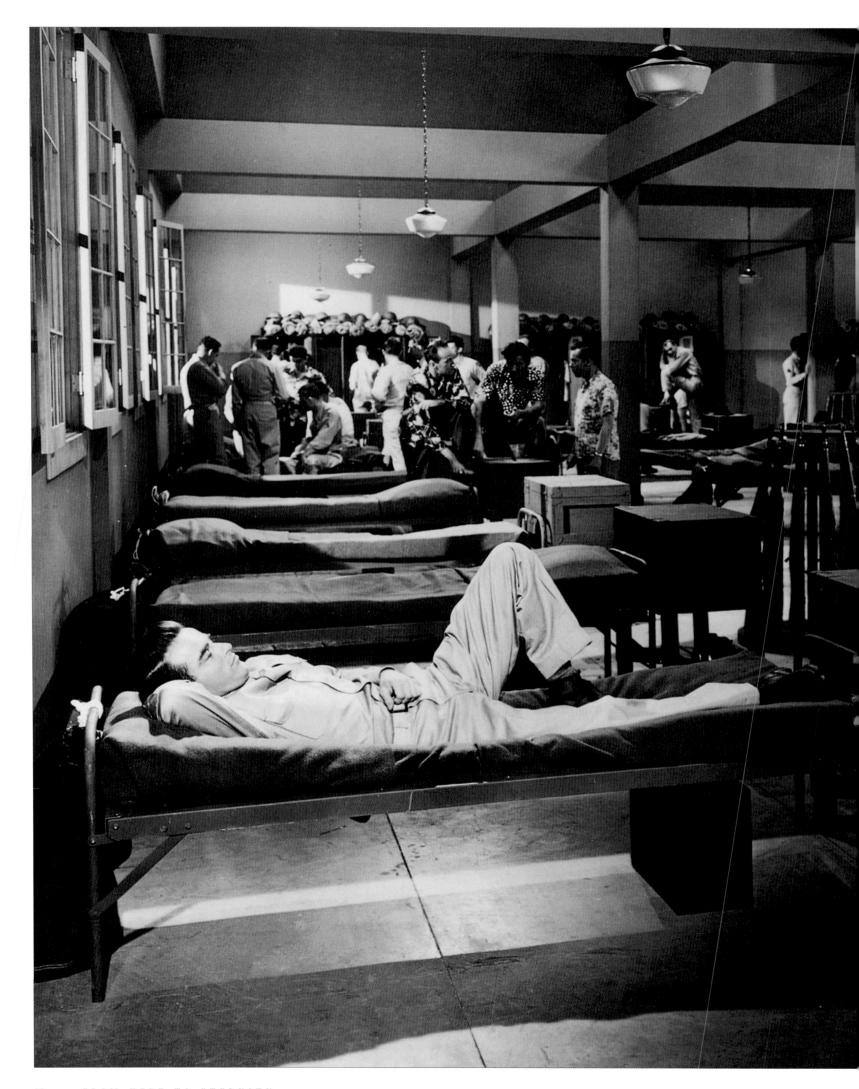

Above: As soon as Frank Sinatra read the screenplay for *From Here to Eternity*, he was convinced that the role of Private Angelo Maggio had been written for him and he began lobbying hard for a chance to audition. At the time, his career was at an all-time low and the film's producer, Harry Cohn, wanted no part of Frank. After some prodding from Ava Gardner, Sinatra was finally able to get a screen test and won the role.

Left: Sinatra with Montgomery Clift in *From Here to Eternity*. Clift was a dedicated, if extremely troubled, actor who threw himself heavily into every role he played. He took Sinatra under his wing and coached him on his every line. "I learned more about acting from Monty [Clift] then I ever knew before," admitted Sinatra. "But he's an exhausting man."

Opposite: In December 1954, Frank and Frank, Jr., walk down First Avenue in New York with Gloria Vanderbilt, who had recently left her husband Maestro Leopold Stokowski. A few years earlier, Sinatra and Vanderbilt had had an affair, but the two remained good friends long after it ended. In 1956, Frank would arrange for Vanderbilt to appear in his movie *Johnny Concho*.

Above: Sinatra jams with Nat "King" Cole in 1955. After signing with Capitol Records in 1953, Frank hooked up with Nat Cole's talented young arranger, Nelson Riddle. The laid-back, swinging style that Riddle had developed with Cole suited Sinatra to a tee, resulting in some of the finest recordings of Frank's career.

ight: By 1954, Sinatra had regained much of the fame he had enjoyed earlier in his career. He was named the most popular male vocalist by *Downbeat* magazine for the first time since 1947. Sinatra was also proving again to be a big draw at the box office with *Young at Heart* (1954), the musical remake of Fannie Hurst's *Four Daughters*, costarring Doris Day (left). The Nelson Riddle–arranged theme song "Young at Heart" was Sinatra's first hit single in seven years, reaching number two on the charts.

ight: Sinatra and his teenage daughter Nancy attend the premiere of the 1955 film *Not as a Stranger*. Although Frank was not present during most of his children's upbringing, his eldest daughter Nancy remained extremely devoted to him. "My father may have left," she once said, "but he never left his family."

elow: Frank shares a mike with songstress Rosemary Clooney in 1955. Clooney once said of Sinatra, "I think that he's been true to himself, no matter if that's good, bad, or indifferent. What you get is whatever his history is at that moment."

Above: Sinatra raises a toast with David Wayne in *The Tender Trap*, one of five movies the singer appeared in 1955. During the recording of the title tune for this movie, Frank stormed out of the recording booth and complained to lyricist/composer Sammy Cahn, "Did you see how high the note is for the last 'love' in the song? How can you expect me to hit such a high note?" To which Cahn replied, "Because you're Frank Sinatra." A furious Sinatra went back into the booth and hit the note perfectly on the next take, all the while glaring at Cahn.

Left: In August 1956, Sinatra returned to the Paramount for a week-long engagement with Tommy Dorsey—fourteen years after leaving his former bandleader. "He's the most fascinating man in the world," Dorsey once said of Sinatra, "but don't stick your hand in the cage." Dorsey died unexpectedly in his sleep just three months after the reunion.

Above: Sinatra appeared with Marlon Brando in *Guys and Dolls* in 1955. Frank had wanted to play the role of Sky Masterson—Brando's part—in the musical and believed it would have been a better film had he and Brando switched parts. The year before, Brando had won the Best Actor Oscar for his portrayal of Terry Malloy in *On the Waterfront*, a role that Sinatra had coveted.

Left: Sinatra gave one of his greatest acting performances as the heroin-addicted card dealer Frankie Machine in *The Man with the Golden Arm* (1955), directed by Otto Preminger and costarring Eleanor Parker, Kim Novak, and Darren McGavin. This was one of Sinatra's own personal favorites, and it earned him a Best Actor nomination.

Right: Otto Preminger, standing behind the cameraman, shows Sinatra how to yawn, during the filming of *The Man with the Golden Arm*. Sinatra jokingly referred to the Austrian movie director as "Ludwig." Both Sinatra and Preminger would later take stands against Hollywood blacklisting by hiring writers who were part of the Hollywood Ten, a group of screenwriters called to testify about the influence of communism in Hollywood. Preminger hired Dalton Trumbo to write *Exodus* (1960) and Sinatra hired Albert Maltz to write a version of *The Execution of Private Slovik*, which was never actually made.

Above: By the time he appeared with Bing Crosby (far left) and Grace Kelly (in Frank's arms) in *High Society* in 1956, Frank Sinatra had become the number-one box-office draw in Hollywood.

Left: Sinatra with Sophia Loren in the 1957 film, *The Pride and the Passion*, directed by Stanley Kramer. Kramer, who directed Sinatra in the 1955 film *Not as a Stranger*, had vowed never to use him again after Frank, Robert Mitchum, and Broderick Crawford got drunk and destroyed a dressing room. Against his better judgment, he hired Frank for *The Pride and the Passion*, and the director and the moody actor were at constant loggerheads during the sixteen-week shoot in Spain. Sinatra was also at odds with his other costar, Cary Grant.

Right: Sinatra strikes a classic pose in *The Joker is Wild* (1957). Frank began seeing Lauren Bacall during the filming of this movie, even though Bacall's husband and Sinatra's good friend, Humphrey Bogart, was dying of cancer at the time. One year after Bogart's death and about a year and a half after Frank's divorce from Ava, Sinatra proposed to Bacall. When Bacall's agent, Swifty Lazaar, leaked news of Sinatra's engagement to Bacall to the press, Frank immediately dropped her and didn't speak to her again for six years.

Right: In 1957, Sinatra signed a three-year, three-million-dollar contract with ABC to film thirty-six half-hour television shows. ABC was hoping that *The Frank Sinatra Show* would pull the "third network" out of its ratings doldrums. However, Frank, who had always hated to rehearse, rushed through eleven shows in thirteen days and showed little interest in conquering television. The show was dropped after twenty-six weeks. Here, Sinatra performs with Bing Crosby, left, and Dean Martin, right.

Left: Sinatra with Kim Novak in *Pal Joey* (1957). Novak was one of many actresses with whom Sinatra was romantically involved over the years. Others included Marilyn Maxwell, Gloria Vanderbilt, Marilyn Monroe, Juliet Prowse, and Natalie Wood.

Left: Shirley MacLaine got an early career boost when Frank Sinatra gave her a part in *Some Came Running* (1958), and then had the character changed to suit her talents. MacLaine received her first Academy Award nomination for her role as Sinatra's wife, and she later became the only woman to be admitted to Sinatra's notorious Rat Pack.

Below: Sinatra with Dean Martin in *Some Came Running*. Directed by Vincente Minelli, the film was based on the controversial novel by James Jones, who was also the author of *From Here to Eternity*.

Right: Shirley MacLaine, shown here with Frank in *Some Came Running*, once said of Sinatra's acting, "His potential is fantastic. The thing is, I wish he would work harder at what he's doing….He doesn't even like to rehearse….Maybe he's afraid to see what might happen if he worked up to his whole potential. It might destroy everything he's done by playing it casual."

Left: Frank Sinatra and Sammy Davis, Jr. share a few laughs at a costume benefit at the Moulin Rouge nightclub in Hollywood. Later that night in the parking lot of the club, an intoxicated Sinatra got into separate altercations with actor John Wayne (because Wayne had criticized Sinatra for hiring a blacklisted writer) and with a parking lot attendant (who nearly hit Sinatra as he stormed off after his confrontation with the Duke).

Left: Frank mans a slot machine in a scene from *Ocean's Eleven* (1960), which was filmed at the Sands and which featured Sinatra's Rat Pack, who were also performing in a stage act at the hotel. On the eve of the November presidential primary, Senator Jack Kennedy flew to Vegas to catch the show. Sinatra introduced Kennedy to Judith Campbell, who was later identified by the Justice Department as a girlfriend of Chicago gangster Sam Giancana. It has been rumored that Giancana collected crucial trade union votes for Kennedy in exchange for cash payments and a promise to ease federal investigations into Mob activities.

Right: On September 19, 1959, Frank Sinatra served as master of ceremonies at a luncheon honoring Soviet Premier Nikita Khrushchev and his wife, Nina, who were making an unprecedented visit to the United States. Here, Sinatra introduces Maurice Chevalier (left) and Louis Jourdan (seated) to the Soviet Premier and his party, who are seated in the balcony.

Chapter Four

Five O'Clock Vegas Blue

Above: Dean Martin and Frank Sinatra attend the opening of Eddie Fisher's act at the Cocoanut Grove in 1961. Frank and Dean had become good friends ever since they had appeared together in the 1958 film *Some Came Running*.

Opposite: By 1960, Frank Sinatra had a lot to smile about. That year the Film Exhibitors of America voted him the Top Box Office Star, he had final say over virtually every movie he made, and he was one of the highest paid performers in Las Vegas. In 1961, he decided to expand the control he had over his own recordings by starting his own record company, Reprise.

A bove: Frank wallows through the muck in a scene from *The Devil at 4 O'Clock* (1961), also starring Spencer Tracy.

Above: The Rat Pack, from left to right: Peter Lawford, Sammy Davis, Jr., Frank Sinatra, Joey Bishop, and Dean Martin. The name Rat Pack (alternately "The Clan") was originally used by Lauren Bacall to describe Humphrey Bogart and his gang of friends, of which Frank was a member. After Bogey's death, Frank formed his own Rat Pack, with himself as the undisputed leader.

Left: Frank was an enthusiastic supporter of John F. Kennedy, campaigning relentlessly for the young senator. He even re-recorded the 1959 song "High Hopes" with new lyrics that championed Kennedy as the answer to the nation's problems. Kennedy, in turn, was enamored of Sinatra's swinging lifestyle and the no-holds-barred attitude of the Rat Pack. After making Kennedy an honorary member of his group, Sinatra even gave the presidential hopeful his own nickname: "Chicky Baby."

STAIR-4

Above: Frank Sinatra escorts Jacqueline Kennedy to the inaugural gala to honor the President-elect the night before his swearing in. Sinatra had been in charge of planning the gala, which raised more than one million dollars to help pay off Kennedy's campaign debt. Jackie reluctantly allowed Sinatra to escort her to the event— she didn't like Frank much at the time. A little over a decade later, however, the two wound up in bed together.

elow (from left to right): Jack Entratter (president of Sands Hotel), Dean Martin, Sammy Davis, Jr., Danny Thomas, Lucille Ball, Frank Sinatra, and Gary Morton celebrate the eleventh anniversary of the Sands Hotel, December 15, 1963.

Above: In *The Manchurian Candidate* (1962), Sinatra played an American soldier who had been brainwashed by Communists and made part of a plan to assassinate the President. The president of United Artists was hesitant to distribute the controversial film until Sinatra went directly to President Kennedy to get his approval.

Right: Sinatra and Janet Leigh in *The Manchurian Candidate*.

Above: Sinatra and the Rat Pack in *Robin and the Seven Hoods* (1964). While filming a graveyard scene for this film, news came over the radio that President Kennedy had been shot. Sinatra immediately halted shooting and went for a solitary, reflective walk. "Two images I remember of Frank," recalled Sammy Davis, Jr. "Frank walking down Broadway in the fifties when nobody recognized him, when he was alone, no hat on, topcoat collar up. And the image of him walking—on that beautiful sunlit day—in a graveyard."

Left: Two weeks after the Kennedy assassination, Sinatra's only son, Frank, Jr., (who had just launched his singing career) was abducted at gunpoint during an engagement at Harrah's Hotel in Lake Tahoe. Here, Frank tells reporters that his son was returned safely for a $240,000 ransom.

Right: In 1965, Sinatra sang eighteen songs in an hour-long NBC special entitled "Sinatra—A Man and His Music." The press release for the show poked fun at the latest rock and roll invasion that was sweeping the country by catering to people who are "tired of kid singers wearing mops of hair thick enough to hide a crate of melons."

Above: In *Von Ryan's Express* (1965) Sinatra plays a colonel who leads his troops out of a POW camp during World War II. It was during the filming of this movie that he met his third wife, Mia Farrow.

Above: In August 1965, Frank Sinatra and nineteen-year-old Mia Farrow (who was thirty years Frank's junior) left for a vacation aboard the 168-foot yacht *Southern Breeze*. The press was in a frenzy over rumors that the two would be married, pursuing them from port to port on the Northeast coast. The vacation was cut short, however, when one of the crewmen drowned off Martha's Vineyard.

Above: Frank and Mia were married in a small ceremony in Las Vegas, July 19, 1966. The marriage would only last a little over thirteen months. Sinatra didn't want Mia to work, and when she accepted the lead role in Roman Polanski's *Rosemary's Baby*, Sinatra had his lawyer serve Mia with divorce papers.

ight: By the end of the six-ties, in such films as *Assault on a Queen* (1966); *The Naked Runner* (1967); *Tony Rome* (1967); *The Detective* (1968); and *Lady in Cement* (1969), Sinatra primarily played tough, hard-boiled characters that mirrored the myth of his off-screen persona. In *Tony Rome*, he continued his tradition of putting friends in his films by finding parts for his lawyer Mickey Rudin and for Shecky Greene, as well as for former girlfriends Jill St. John, Deana Lund, and Tiffany Bolling.

elow: Sinatra with Raquel Welch in *Lady in Cement* (1969). Welch said of Sinatra: "I wouldn't have missed working with Frank for the world. He's an education for any actor—you actually learn how to make everything count. Working with him is exciting. He has a magnetism I've never come across before."

Left: Frank, his daughter Nancy, his ex-wife Nancy, and Frank, Jr. at the opening night of Frank Jr.'s engagement at Caesar's Palace in Las Vegas, 1969. Sinatra was always supportive of both his son's and daughter's choices to pursue singing careers, although he acknowledged that the road would be much harder for Frank, Jr., who would forever be compared to his father.

Right: A scene from one of Sinatra's comedies, *Dirty Dingus Magee* (1970). This was Sinatra's fifty-fifth film; he would not appear again on the big screen for ten years.

Above: Frank Sinatra swings an arm around Count Basie in England, 1970.

Above: On April 15, 1971, Frank Sinatra won a special Oscar, the Jean Hersholt Humanitarian Award, presented by actor Gregory Peck. Less then a month later Sinatra would announce his retirement from show business. He had made fifty-five films, one hundred albums, and more than two thousand individual recordings, and had given countless live performances.

Chapter Five

Ol' Blue Eyes Is Back

Above: In November 1973, Sinatra ended his two-and-a-half-year retirement with an album and a television special titled "Ol' Blue Eyes Is Back." He then began a rigorous touring schedule (140 performances in 1975 alone) that would continue off and on for the next twenty years.

Opposite: Sinatra accepts a rose from a fan at the end of his October 1974 concert at Madison Square Garden. Billed as "The Main Event," this internationally televised concert was perhaps one of the greatest performances of Sinatra's later career—despite the fact that he didn't rehearse for it and showed up at the arena just twenty minutes before going on stage. "I have never felt so much love in one room in my entire life," Sinatra would later say.

Left: President Nixon adjusts the microphone for Sinatra before a performance in the White House in 1973.

Opposite: After years of sordid romances, marriages, and affairs, Frank married his last wife, Barbara Marx, in Rancho Mirage, California, on July 11, 1976. Barbara was the ex-wife of Zeppo Marx of the Marx Brothers.

Right: Frank, with wife Barbara, left, and mother Dolly, right, on the night that he received the SCOPUS Award from the Hebrew University of Israel for Extraordinary Accomplishments in His Chosen Profession and His Dedication to Humanitarian Causes the World Over," November 19, 1976.

Right: Sinatra, second from left, at the Westchester Premier Theater with reputed Mobsters (from left) Gregory DePalma, Thomas Marslow, Carlo Gambino, Jimmy "The Weasel" Fratiano, and (seated in front) Richard "Nerves" Fusco. This 1976 photo would be used as evidence in a federal Mob trial when members of the Gambino crime family were accused of siphoning off concessions money from the Sinatra shows at the theater. (The photograph was printed in newspapers with the identity of the person at bottom left concealed.)

Right: Frank and Barbara are escorted by three Israeli guards armed with M-16 assault rifles to a dedication ceremony at the Hebrew University of Jerusalem, April 9, 1978. Actor Gregory Peck is shown between Frank and Barbara in the background.

Above: Forty years after he hired a skinny, big-eared practically unknown named Frank Sinatra, bandleader Harry James (right) rejoins the singing legend on stage for a rendition of there first hit together, "All or Nothing at All," at the Universal Ampitheatre in Los Angeles on June 16, 1979.

Right: In 1980, Sinatra returned to the big screen after a nearly ten-year hiatus to appear in *The First Deadly Sin* with Faye Dunaway. This would be his last starring role (he had a cameo in *Cannonball Run II* in 1983). Sinatra had wanted to play the role of the alcoholic lawyer in *The Verdict* (1982), but the part went to Paul Newman.

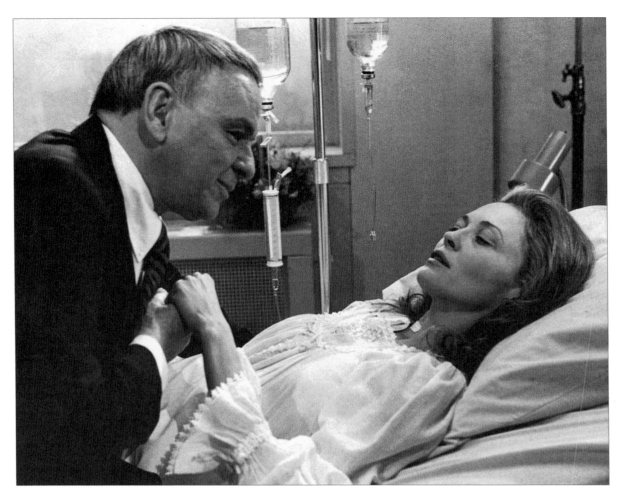

Left and opposite: Later in his life, the longtime liberal Democrat turned decidedly Republican in his politics, developing lasting friendships with Republican politicians. Left, Frank playfully swings Nancy Reagan away from her husband when he tries to cut in during a party at the White House. Opposite, Sinatra performs at the 1981 Inaugural Gala (which he also produced) honoring Ronald Reagan. Twenty years earlier he had produced a similar event for John F. Kennedy. Sinatra had formed a friendship with Richard Nixon after Nixon won the election in 1968, and in 1972, he supported the Nixon–Agnew ticket. He helped raise money for President Ford's campaign as well.

ight: Sinatra croons with big band legend Count Basie during the taping of the 1981 television special "Frank Sinatra: The Man and His Music." The NBC special fared poorly in ratings despite the fact that the singer's first album in five years, *Trilogy*, had turned gold in a matter of weeks just two years before.

Left: Steve Lawrence and Edie Gorme perform with Frank at the end of his seventy-fifth birthday concert at the Meadowlands Arena in East Rutherford, New Jersey.

Right: Frank Sinatra was honored by the NAACP with a Lifetime Achievement Award in May 1987. Here, the entertainer is joined by boxing great Sugar Ray Robinson, who presented the award.

Above: Longtime Sinatra friend Rosalind Russell once asked the singer if he could count the number of benefits he had performed in over the years. He just laughed. Here, Frank performs with Liza Minelli at a benefit concert for San Diego State University's general athletic fund in 1988.

Opposite: Sinatra poses with his National Broadcasters Hall of Fame Award, one of countless awards he received over the years.

Above: The Rat Pack is back. In 1988, Frank Sinatra, Dean Martin, and Sammy Davis, Jr., embarked on a twenty-nine-city tour to help pull Martin out of the depression he'd been in since his son, Dino, Jr., died in a plane crash the year before. Here, the trio gathers around the piano in Davis' house for an informal rehearsal.

Above: Continuing his practice later in life of supporting Republican candidates, Sinatra pulled for George Bush at the 1988 GOP convention in New Orleans. Here, Frank works the convention with his wife Barbara and Henry Kissinger.

Right: Sinatra receives the Tower of Achievement Award from Capitol Records, November 7, 1993. Frank's Capitol recordings between 1953 and 1962, including *In the Wee Small Hours* (1955) and *Come Fly With Me* (1958), were some of the most influential and artistically successful of his entire career.

Left: Although his voice sometimes faltered and he occasionally had trouble remembering the words, Frank Sinatra continued to wow audiences with his live performances almost right up until his death. In 1993 and 1994 he recorded his last two albums, *Duets* and *Duets II,* on which he sang with (among others) Barbra Streisand, Tony Bennett, Aretha Franklin, Julio Iglesias, Gloria Estefan, and Bono from the rock group U2. After a career that touched seven decades and had countless peaks and valley, Francis Albert Sinatra could still make a hit record.

Left: For his eightieth birthday celebration, Frank Sinatra appeared in his final television special, "Sinatra: 80 Years My Way." This special was taped live at the Shrine Auditorium in Los Angeles, and aired on December 14, 1995—two days after his actual birthday. Here, Frank cuts into his birthday cake at a party at the Hilton in New York City.

Conclusion

Left: Singer. Actor. Political activist. Frank Sinatra enjoyed a career that spanned more than fifty years.

Speculation as to why Sinatra initially retired ranged from rumors that his health was failing to a belief that he was depressed after the death of his father in January 1971. From his home in Palm Springs, Sinatra issued a statement saying that he needed an "opportunity for reflection, reading, self-examination...a long pause to seek a better understanding of changes occurring in the world." Who could blame Sinatra for wanting to retire? After all, he had been at it for more than thirty years and had accomplished just about everything a performer could hope to have accomplished. He was universally accepted as one of the greatest pop singers in history—as well as one of show business' most colorful personalities.

Sinatra's farewell concert was scheduled for June 13, 1971. The event was carefully planned by Sinatra himself. He wanted to go out with the same style and grace that had become his trademark. Some of the biggest names in show business appeared at the event: Barbra Streisand, Pearl Bailey, Jack Benny, Bob Hope, Cary Grant, Gregory Peck, Don Rickles, and, of course, Sammy Davis, Jr. The show went on for nearly four hours before Sinatra appeared. A

little past midnight, a tearful Rosalind Russell introduced Frank for what was supposed to be his final performance: "Our friend has made a decision, a decision we don't particularly like, but one which we must honor. He's worked long and hard for thirty years with his head and his voice and especially his heart...."

And with that Frank Sinatra took the stage to the frenzied cheers of the standing-room-only crowd. He performed a thirty-minute set that night that allayed anyone's worries about his health. In strong voice he sang "All or Nothing at All," "I'll Never Smile Again," "I've Got You Under My Skin," "The Lady Is a Tramp," "Ol' Man River," and "My Way." And then, with the stage darkened except for one small spotlight, he sang his last song, the smoky saloon ballad "Angel Eyes." As the song drew to a close, he lit a cigarette, paused, and sang the last line, "Excuse me while I disappear."

As dramatic and well choreographed as that exit was, it was far from Sinatra's final appearance. By 1973, he was ready for yet another comeback. In November, Sinatra planned his glorious return to show business with a televised concert and a new album, both appropriately titled *Ol' Blue Eyes Is Back*. Frank Sinatra would

Left: Sinatra thanks his audience for their devotion at his eightieth birthday celebration at the Shrine Auditorium.

never again officially retire. In concert tours with such extravagant names as "The Main Event," "The Ultimate Event," and "The Diamond Jubilee World Tour," Sinatra kept working and remained very much in the public eye. Although Frank didn't record with quite as much frequency in the last twenty-plus years of his career, such albums as *The Main Event*, *Trilogy*, *L.A. Is My Lady*, *Duets*, and *Duets II* proved that even later in life, Frank Sinatra was still a force in popular music.

In the last year of his life, Sinatra's health declined rapidly. He was hospitalized, suffering from a variety of ailments including pneumonia, a heart attack, kidney problems, and Alzheimer's disease, but each time he fought back. As Frank himself once said, "You gotta love livin', dyin' is a pain in the ass."

Sinatra provided the soundtrack to the lives of millions of people, and as his career went on, newer and newer generations discovered the wonders of "The Voice." At Sinatra's eightieth birthday celebration at the Shrine Auditorium in Los Angeles, fellow New Jersey native Bruce Springsteen paid fitting tribute to the American legend: "[Sinatra's] was a voice filled with bad attitude, life, beauty, excitement...and a sad knowledge of the world....It was the deep bluesness of Frank's voice that affected me the most, and, while his music became synonymous with black tie, good life, the best booze, women, sophistication, his blues voice was always the sound of hard luck and men late at night with the last ten dollars in their pockets trying to figure a way out. On behalf of all New Jersey, Frank, I want to say, 'Hail, brother, you sang out your soul.'"

Filmography

Las Vegas Nights, Paramount, 1941

Ships Ahoy, MGM, 1942

Reveille with Beverly, Columbia, 1943

Higher and Higher, RKO, 1943

Step Lively, RKO, 1943

Anchors Aweigh, MGM, 1945

The House I Live In, RKO, 1945

Till the Clouds Roll By, MGM, 1946

It Happened in Brooklyn, MGM, 1947

The Miracle of the Bells, RKO, 1948

The Kissing Bandit, MGM, 1948

Take Me Out to the Ball Game, MGM, 1949

On the Town, MGM, 1949

Double Dynamite, RKO, 1951

Meet Danny Wilson, Universal-International, 1951

From Here to Eternity, Columbia, 1953

Suddenly, Libra Production/United Artists Release, 1954

Young at Heart, Arwin Production/Warner Brothers Release, 1955

Not as a Stranger, Stanley Kramer Production/United Artists Release, 1955

The Tender Trap, MGM, 1955

Guys and Dolls, Samuel Goldwyn/MGM Release, 1955

The Man with the Golden Arm, Carlyle Production/United Artists Release, 1955

Meet Me in Las Vegas, MGM, 1956

Johnny Concho, Kent Production/United Artists Release, 1956

High Society, MGM, 1956

Around the World in 80 Days, Michael Todd Production/United Artists Release, 1956

The Pride and the Passion, Stanley Kramer Production/Paramount Release, 1957

The Joker is Wild, M.B.L. Production/Paramount Release, 1957

Pal Joey, Essex-George Sidney Production/Columbia Release, 1957

Kings Go Forth, Frank Ross-Eton Production/United Artist Release, 1958

Some Came Running, MGM, 1958

A Hole in the Head, Sincap Production/United Artist Release, 1959

Never So Few, Canterbury Production/MGM Release, 1959

Can-Can, Suffolk-Cummings Production/Twentieth Century-Fox Release, 1960

Ocean's Eleven, Dorchester Production/Warner Brothers Release, 1960

Pepe, G.S. Posa Films International/Columbia Release, 1960

The Devil at 4 O'Clock, Columbia, 1961

Sergeants 3, Essex-Claude Production/United Artist Release, 1962

The Road to Hong Kong, Melnor Films Production/United Artist Release, 1962

The Manchurian Candid.ate, M.C. Production/United Artists Release, 1963

Come Blow Your Horn, Essex-Tandem Production/Paramount Release, 1963

The List of Adrian Messenger, Joel Production/Universal Release, 1963

4 for Texas, Sam Company Production/Warner Brothers Release, 1964

Robin and the Seven Hoods, P-C Production\Warner Brothers, 1964

None But the Brave, Artanis Production/Warner Brothers Release, 1965

Von Ryan's Express, P-R Production/Twentieth Century-Fox Release, 1965

Marriage on the Rocks, A-C Production/Warner Brothers, Release, 1965

Cast a Giant Shadow, Mirisch-Llenroc-Batjack Production/United Artists Release, 1965

The Oscar, Greene-Rouse Production/Embassy Release, 1966

Assault on a Queen, Sinatra Enterprises-Seven Arts Production/Paramount Release, 1966

The Naked Runner, Sinatra Enterprises Production/Warner Brothers Release, 1967

Tony Rome, Arcola-Millfield Production/Twentieth Century-Fox Release, 1967

The Detective, Arcola-Millfeld Production/Twentieth Century-Fox Release, 1968

Lady in Cement, Arcola-Millfield Production/Twentieth Century-Fox Release, 1968

Dirty Dingus Magee, MGM, 1970

Contract on Cherry Street (made-for-TV), Atlantis Production/Columbia Release, 1977

The First Deadly Sin, Atlantis-Cinema VII Production/Filmways Release, 1980

Cannonball Run II, Warner Brothers, 1984

Discography
(Albums Only)

Song for Young Lovers, Capital, 1954

Swing Easy, Capital, 1954

In the Wee Small Hours, Capital, 1957

Songs for Swingin Lovers, Capital, 1956

Close to You, Capital, 1957

A Swingin' Affair, Capital, 1957

Where Are You?, Capital, 1957

A Jolly Christmas from Frank Sinatra, Capital, 1957

Come Fly with Me, Capital, 1958

Only the Lonely, Capital, 1958

Come Dance with Me, Capital, 1959

Look to Your Heart, Capital, 1959

No One Cares, Capital, 1959

Nice 'n' Easy, Capital, 1960

Sinatras Swingin' Session, Capital, 1961

All the Way, Capital, 1961

Come Swing with Me, Capital, 1961
Ring-A-Ding-Ding, Reprise, 1961
Sinatra Swings, Reprise, 1961
I Remember Tommy, Reprise, 1961
Point of No Return, Capital, 1962
Sinatra Sings of Love and Things, Capital,
    1962
Sinatra and Strings, Reprise, 1962
Sinatra and Swingin' Brass, Reprise, 1962
All Alone, Reprise, 1962
Sinatra-Basie, Reprise, 1963
The Concert Sinatra, Reprise, 1963
Sinatra's Sinatra, Reprise, 1963
Frank Sinatra Sings Days of Wine and Roses,
    Moon River and other Academy Award
Winners, Reprise, 1964
Sinatra-Basie: It Might as Well Be Swing,
    Reprise, 1964
Softly, As I Leave You, Reprise, 1964
Sinatra 65, Reprise, 1965
September of My Years, Reprise, 1965
A Man and His Music, Reprise, 1965
My Kind of Broadway, Reprise, 1965
Moonlight Sinatra, Reprise, 1966
Strangers in the Night, Reprise, 1966
Sinatra-Basie: Sinatra at the Sands, Reprise,
    1966
That's Life, Reprise, 1966
Francis Albert Sinatra & Antonio Carlos Jobim,
    Reprise, 1967
Frank Sinatra and Frank & Nancy, Reprise,
    1967
Francis A. & Edward K., Reprise, 1968
Cycles, Reprise, 1968
My Way, Reprise, 1969
A Man Alone, Reprise, 1969
Watertown, Reprise, 1970
Sinatra & Company, Reprise, 1971
Ol Blue Eyes Is Back, Sinatra, 1973
Some Nice Things I've Missed, 1974
The Main Event/Live from Madison Square
    Garden, Reprise, 1974
Trilogy, Reprise, 1980
She Shot Me Down, Reprise, 1S~8 1
L.A. Is My Lady, Quest, 1984
Duets, Capitol, 1993
Duets II, Capitol, 1994

Recommended Collections
Reprise Collection, Warner Brothers, 1990
Capitol Years, Capitol, 1990
Sinatra 80th Live, Capitol, 1995
Sinatra 80thAll the Best, Capitol, 1995
The Best of the Columbia Years, Sony, 1995
The Complete Capitol Singles Collection,
    Capitol, 1997

Bibliography

Davis, Sammy Jr., Hollywood in a Suitcase.
    New York: William Morrow and
    Company, Inc., 1980.

Gardner, Ava. Ava, My Story. New York:
    Bantam Books, 1990.

Howlett, John Frank Sinatra. New York:
    Simon & Schuster, 1979.

Irwin, Lew. Sinatra: The Pictorial Biography.
    New York: Friedman/Fairfax, 1995.

Jewell, Derek. Frank Sinatra. Boston: Little,
    Brown, 1985.

Kelly, Kitty. His Way: The Unauthorized
    Biography of Frank Sinatra. New York:

Bantam, 1986.

Petkov, Steven and Leonard Mustazza, eds.
    The Frank Sinatra Reader. Oxford
    University Press, 1995.

Rockwell, John. Sinatra, An American Classic.
    New York: Rolling Stone Press, 1984.

Shaw, Arnold. Sinatra: The Entertainer. New
    York: Putnam, 1982.

Sinatra, Nancy. Frank Sinatra, My Father.
    New York: Doubleday & Company,
    1985.

Sinatra, Nancy. Frank Sinatra, An American
    Legend. New York: General Publishing
    Group, 1995.

Index